Photographers:
Paula Oudman, cover, cd and pages 6, 7, 8, 9, 10, 11, 12, 13, 14, 15, 16, 17, 18, 19, 20, 23, 24, 25, 26, 30, 32, 33, 34, 36, 37, 46, 47, 49, 53, 57, 59, 60, 61, 62, 63, 66, 70, 71, 72, 73, 75, 76, 77, 78, 79, 80, 81, 82, 83, 88;
Francesco Cito, pages 27, 38, 40, 41, 42, 44, 48, 50, 54, 56, 58, 68, 74, 84;
Aldo Bianchi, pages 4, 22, 28, 29, 45, 52, 64, 67

ISBN: 978-88-6350-001-1

Art Direction and Design by Marco Pennisi & C.

Produced, printed and manufactured by optimal media production GmbH, Robel/Germany

earBOOKS is a division of edel entertainment GmbH

For more information about earBOOKS please visit www.earbooks.net

Marrakech

MEDERSA BEN YOUSSEF

RESTAURANT ARGANA

الحرير الهندي

1151

52

ARGANA
أركانة

Restaurant
HOTEL

13

Pampers

7

HONDA
LEAD

CD 1

1. Entering Sahara 1.46
2. Bahr Belà Mà 5.39
3. Indigo Turban 4.32
4. The Agadez Cross 4.22
5. Azalai: Caravans Of Salt 5.10
6. Marrakech Sounds & Visions Pt. 1 10.59
7. Marrakech Sounds & Visions Pt. 2 9.53

All songs by Luca Saporiti - Publisher Lagash Edizioni Musicali Srl/Edel Music s.r.l.
Except Trk. 6/7 songs by Massimo Villa - Publisher Edel Music s.r.l.

CD 2

1. Mirages And Oasis Hidden In Dunes 3.44
2. The Rhythm Of Tassili N'ajjer 4.32
3. Start Walking Again 3.44
4. Amenokal, Head Of The Tribes 2.40
5. Memoirs Of Imohag: The Free Men 5.21
6. Marrakech Sounds & Visions Pt. 3 8.04
7. Marrakech Sounds & Visions Pt. 4 15.39

All songs by Luca Saporiti - Publisher Lagash Edizioni Musicali Srl/Edel Music s.r.l.
Except Trk. 6/7 songs by Massimo Villa - Publisher Edel Music s.r.l.